www.finishinglinepress.com

eyes that look with sun but see with moon

poems by

Jack Greene

Finishing Line Press
Georgetown, Kentucky

eyes that look with sun but see with moon

For my Mother and Father

Lila Greene (1932-2010) Mel Greene (1927-2005)

For my first chord of flesh

Day Russ Deb Bob

And for my second

Lisa Mila Maedée Julea

ACKNOWLEDGMENTS

"Mimesis" published in *Lilliput Review*
"Perfect" and "Kaddish for my Father" published in *not enough night*
"Where French Fries Come From," "Untitled Parenthetically," "Sublunary Ice
Cream" published *Mungo vs Ranger*
"Why Not," "Dans l'ensemble," "Along the Shore," published *Bombay Gin*
"An Old Man Finds an Old List," "Eating an Apple During an Extended
Depression," and "Poem Beginning and Ending with Lines from the Emerald
Table" published in *Rattapallax*
"About Suffering We Were Always Wrong" and "Prayer to Ariadne"
published in *Sextant Review*

Thank you to all of my teachers and fellow poets and writers and artists at
Naropa and NYC—all of you, "figures of outward." Thank you to my family
and friends who from time to time would ask how the book was coming
along. And Lisa, life partner, every step of the way, thank you my love.

Publisher: Leah Huete de Maines
Editor: Christen Kincaid
Cover Art: Jack Greene
Author Photo: Lisa Trank
Cover Design: Elizabeth Maines McCleavy

Order online: www.finishinglinepress.com
also available on amazon.com

Author inquiries and mail orders:
Finishing Line Press
PO Box 1626
Georgetown, Kentucky 40324
USA

Contents

Prefix (a cut-up of Guest)

Like paragraphs
we enter—

night
a bridge
balance
a listening

a pear
that
drops

seamless rifts
overhead
the rhythm
of trees

such
is the promise

Untitled, Parenthetically

Imagination, an instinct
in which the world
becomes itself again—
not in like but in kind

as when a deer
at the edge of
a table left
for wood in a forest

seeks not a chair
but its shadow

Simulacrum at the Natural History Museum

Lit from above
a drop of shellac
on a deer's nose
brings her back:

her nose, moist
sniffs frozen air
ears—tall—stiff
hear what

eyes confirm:
danger's last image
approaching
the glass

Mimesis

Though clouds
quickly pass
from my window

see how faithfully
they stay with me,
here, at my desk—

a pulpy-white
sunlit burst
of mimesis

Vermeer's Aquarium

Nothing interrupts the light in Vermeer's studio

Outside his window
there were three
wars with England
the Reformation
and Counter-Reformation

Inside, people sit
like fish in
morning light

the bliss of drapes
chairs high walls
maps and tables—

solid things
that breathe
from floor
to ceiling

We stare into Vermeer's aquarium
like pilgrims at a shrine:

Approaching the canvas
we find certainty
in the light—

like Proust in his cork-lined room
like Cornell in his glass cases
like deer at a lake at dawn

Along the Shore

"The intuitive is not discarded"
—Lisa Hammond

Along the shore
                sea shells
along your bed
                kelp and vine—
waves from a place
only you could see

I heard your voice in Florence
along the banks of the Arno
in the 14th gallery of the Uffizi
You were there, as before,
long hair, skin of alabaster,
standing on a shell

Water, you said
is not a word

remember water
is

remember water

remember

Poem Beginning and Ending with Lines from
The Emerald Tablet

The Sun is its Father and the Moon is its Mother
Father's heat burns the flesh of all things

At night I carry what remains
down to a lake, dip charred bones

In water cooled by the moon,
listen as the hiss of all things

Returns to sky, cloud, sun and rain:
Thus is the world created

Its force or power is entire
if it is turned into earth;

Ariadne takes the unburned flesh
of darkness, and offers it to the Sun

What's given back is hers—
a single thread of moonlight

spins lightly in the sky
Thus is the world created

Field Notes from a Fallout Shelter

1

Inside the circle
six triangles—

three up
three down—

intersect a single
point

2

triangles pointing down—
full force of bomb's logic
Sphinx of fire
the pyramids
upside down—
the eternity before;

triangles pointing up—
pyramids rising out of fire
the third side open
destroyed
implied by circle's logic—
the eternity afterwards:

FALLOUT

3

this
is the
end of
time

the end
of all
forgiving

no cheeks
left to turn
no teeth
left to rot
no eyes
left to burn
no ears
left to hear
no mouth
left to speak
no sky
left to see
no water
left to drink
no grass
left to grow
no birds
left to fly
no olive branch
left to find
no ark no rainbow
no covenant

nothing
nothing
nothing

Perfect

I use these terms all day
I have to. We all do.
Without them you'd know how I am
and I'd know how you are
and then—
where would we be?

So we say, as often as possible,
it's all good, no worries, not
a problem, it's my bad
(hoping to keep
Hiroshima
under our tongues)

perfect

Sublunary Ice Cream

This new moon
its wick bent
back and forth

scooped a rolling
cone of sun
along its lips

long after
yours
are gone

Extempore Effusion After Reading Steven Taylor's *Loveland*

so much the world
    we wish it
        kinder

that more people
    heard with *what*
        than that

that eye let ear
    be spent by
        love, not fear

what's open
    drums a fallen
        tree that flew

soft so the earlobe
    what's as rain as
        through

Why Not?

It's a seventy-threeish sort of day
vaguely iambic, decasyllabic,
but by no means pentameter. Rain
and its quality have been strained—
changed by soot and other stuff we throw
up to the air. What won't float we flush
to the sea. It's a seventy-threeish
sort of day—degrees sonnet that is, old Shake
himself. The sky's wet & pulpy grey, the trees
pews for birds. But that choir's all gone. Now
the Muse signs her name at the bottom
of the page, gets paid for what's hers.
Sonnets? Why not I say, let's go out and play
It's a seventy-threeish sort of day.

An Old Man Finds an Old List
for Russ

Somewhere, deep in the pockets
of an old jacket
not worn in all the years
since you left it hanging
my hands found folded in a square
a grocery list you once jotted down
in the snow
under a street light
on the way
to the corner store:

lemon
butter
fish
lettuce
onions
bread
tinfoil
Drano

That night
your hands sought
warmth in these
same pockets

and I remember
as I reached
to wipe the snow
from your face

one particular smile
I have not seen
since we discussed
the virtues
of having a list

Where French Fries Come From

halfway between
the familiar
red box and
a sagging mound
of ketchup
one skinny-fingered
french fry
is held above
the usual plunge:

along the edge
of one otherwise
perfectly rendered
golden-thin
salt-engendered
fry
a thread
of antiquity
remains unravished:

a slight yet
certain trace
of brown—

a footnote
to the earth

pure joy
cherished bliss
for those of us
deprived of myth

Träumerei

Some nights just before I fall asleep my mother's wedding veil unravels into a beam of light. On the ceiling is a home movie—the only sounds are clicks and whirrs, and a fan that keeps the film from burning

Pressed forever on the scene is my father's misplaced thumb, a flesh white crescent filling up half the screen. Despite this intrusion, there's still room for a close up—me stuffing my teenage face with a handful of fries. The camera pulls away revealing my brothers in the back seat with me. We are taking turns with a bag of fries. Above my shoulder our dog stands with one foot on the armrest and the other on my arm. Her nose is out the window. She smells everything but fries

The camera pans up to the front seat. Behind the wheel is Mom. Her lips are moving. Save some fries for later. We all laugh, especially Mom. Next to her my sisters also have a bag of fries. My mother's right hand drifts from the wheel to the bag of fries. My sisters help her find what she wants. She smiles. Her eyes never leave the road

The camera cuts to the back to find me pulling up a fry from the seat. I stare into the camera, french fry dangling. I offer it to my father behind the camera which moves left to right and back, indicating *no*. I brush a few hairs off the fry and swallow it whole

A long shot from the far back shows us laughing. The camera shakes a bit, proof Dad was laughing too. A last turn up the hill and we're home, wiping salt and grease off our lips as Mom parks the car on the street, leaving the driveway clear for us to shoot baskets until the film crackles and the ceiling turns to white

My father the camera

is always clicking away
hoping to hold what
he never can find

come to the prow
father, leave the camera
behind

be here with us

Chord of Flesh
for Skip

With a wave
          behind us
          you hold up
the youngest
          your arms firm around him
          your legs strong
          your feet—
                    glazed with sea water—
                    push
                    through sand

We stand five firm
          a chord of flesh
                    along the shore

     the wave frozen   mute

That old dream
          sung by the sea
how each of us
carries it
differently

That long wave
of song—
how you still carry it
how *it*
still carries you

How to fly
          float
turn away
                    come back

Old dreams
shed myth—
new wings
new skin

a new myth
born *now*
as that wave
melts back
to the sea

this myth—
this *now*—

still faithful
to what brought
us here

but closer
to water
freer   as wind

passing—

`   like light

Kaddish

father's foot
cut
through water

kept its
beat
in water

cherished
warmth
of water

pouring down
on him, draining
under him—*out*

through
water
into

song

where one
belongs—

song

house on hill
sky and sea

song

sun and moon
leaf on tree

song

father's foot
a constant

song

even now
with him
gone

song

father lived
and died
in

song

sing on
old man
sing on

Eating an Apple During an Extended Depression

Approaching the core
I stare with old knowledge
longing for seeds in
sleepy white chambers—

shapes that float
from their wells, those
perfect beginnings
that hang at the lip

A child, I didn't
swallow the seeds
afraid a tree
would grow inside me

I swallow the core
impervious to any
myth of apple

knowing if I could imagine
what a child once feared

trees would sprout
out of rocks

Time

for Lisa

The theme
is always
time—

the shape
it takes the
form
it *makes*

so that
at a place
in time
I waited

You walked
through a
wake of
petals

a form cut
out
of time
into space

One form
torn
bends toward
another

as now
time grows
round
inside you

There—
a fish
of human
spine

half-yours
half-mine
all hers'
all time's

The rose
went
lovely

It comes
to go
again

Now let
us
follow

Statue of Ariel and Prospero Facing the Storm

Soaked with a late May storm
I watch the small rain
fall from
Ariel's eyes
                down
        cheeks

arms
        finger-
                tips

        each

drop

        re-
                placed
        with
    a-
                noth-
        er

—AIDS Walk 1992
Delacorte Theatre
Central Park, NYC

Dans l'ensemble
for John Davis (1950-1995)

Once released
a bubble will
rise—perhaps
according
to a certain
pace or wind
yet this much
is certain:

before it
bursts
back into air
it will tingle
sheer thimbles
of delight—
without a single
patch or tear

Envoi

The blessed rags you walk upon dear friend—
a spontaneous ensemble of old magic—
lurk lustfully, somewhere in the air

About Suffering We Were Always Wrong

We still heard the screams from the school as we got back
on the ship and sailed away fast as we could
remembering not to look back on what masters
would paint again as a blood swollen sky

About suffering we were always wrong

Valentine's Ash Wednesday What impact on us
the living who knew none of them
their faces their names their sisters their brothers
who woke up Wednesday like us but ended up dead?

About suffering we were always wrong

That it happens where you work where you eat
where you pray where you sleep
where you run where you teach
where you're smothered in the street

While the rest of us somehow continue
on board the ship   our eyes and ears shut
sailing even deeper into the labyrinth
About suffering we were always wrong

Prayer to Ariadne

Call it an altar—
a place of breath
ladder and brick

wordless wings
above metal—
                    what sings

II

oh let there
be faces
again

various petals
            forsaken cries
the unnoticed
        all

the poet's
hands ears eyes—
        small

III

this is the center
center we seek
center we share
center we *are*:

the body
beautiful body we are
perishable flesh
                        we are

IV

When you hear the word vermin
know you are close—
close to the thing itself
close
to what kills   close to what they are

what they deny
what they once were
also

Hath not
Hath not
Hath not

Hath not everyone
        everything
                eyes?

V

They don't kill us because they fear they are bodies
They kill us because we pretend to have bodies
Bodies that resemble theirs. Too close too near
to what they believe they alone possess—
Therefore we lie; therefore, *vermin*, we are. That which invades
That which must die

VI

Great thing of us forgot
the Temple: not the one
we made and they
destroyed
but the one
we were given—

the one we destroyed:

> that blue of earth
>> those white swirls of cloud
>>> those scattered bits of land

VII

Build me a skylight—
one like the sky
at the end of exile

when the tongue returns
to the mouth and the soul
cries out what it knows:

that we too have been complicit
in the great secret, the off stage
oath that knows but has no time—

even though all day we hear
the sound of ice
breaking
the sound of flesh
dying

sound of sound of sound of
everything at once

Coda: Sun and Moon, Moon and Sun

for the marriage of Debra Greene and David McCloskey

Where the sun and moon
may have been
is unimportant:

what mattered
was the man
before her eyes

and the knowledge
that the light
in his came in
part from hers

eyes that look
with sun but
see with
moon

joined together
near the bottom
of the earth

perfect flesh
along the shore—

sun and moon
moon and sun
sharing light
making light

eyes of
moon
and sun

Notes

Prefix: (a cut-up of Guest) is a cut-up of Barbara Guest's "Illyria," from her collection *Moscow Mansions*

Section V of "Prayer to Ariadne" is indebted to John Berger's essay "The Hour of Poetry" from his book *The Sense of Sight*

Section VI of "Prayer to Ariadne" is dedicated to my brother Bob

Jack Greene is a poet and photographer. A son of a singer and a writer, he was born in Miami Beach, Florida. After graduating from UCLA with a degree in English, he headed to New York City to pursue his poetry career until he felt the call of the Rocky Mountains and received his MFA in Writing and Poetics at Naropa University in Boulder, Colorado. He is the past recipient of a Colorado Council on the Arts Poetry Fellowship and served as poet-in-residence for the Colorado Council on the Arts. He has taught poetry and creative writing workshops and courses in the Front Range. His photography has been exhibited at Naropa University, the Boulder Jewish Community Center, and the University of Colorado, Boulder. His fine art photography can be seen at jackgreenephotography. picfair.com. He lives in Longmont, Colorado with the writer and performer Lisa Trank.